Standish O'Grady

The Crisis in Ireland

Standish O'Grady

The Crisis in Ireland

ISBN/EAN: 9783337325664

Printed in Europe, USA, Canada, Australia, Japan

Cover: Foto ©ninafisch / pixelio.de

More available books at **www.hansebooks.com**

IN

IRELAND.

BY

STANDISH O'GRADY,

*Late Honorary Secretary of Landlords' Meeting in the Rotunda,
December 22, 1881.*

DUBLIN:

PONSONBY, 113 GRAFTON STREET.

LONDON: SIMPKIN AND MARSHALL.

———

1882.

THE CRISIS IN IRELAND.

THE political and social horizon to-day in
Ireland is, at least for one class, and for
the friends and sympathisers of that class,
overcast and gloomy in the extreme. Yet
dark and stormy as the outlook is now, it will
be yet darker and stormier. A lull more
apparent than real may at this moment prevail, but the lull is only of thunder and of the
noisy and innocuous wind; for, meanwhile,
strong tides, which no force can stem, bear
closer and ever closer to an iron-bound shore
the little fleet in which are embarked the
persons and fortunes of the Irish Landlords,
and the many interests and hopes of which
they are the centre. The mass meetings are
at an end, the platform is silent, but the
spirit of which they were the manifestation

is here still unexorcised. The fierce oratory of the incipient revolution is no longer heard, or heard only in muttered curses and the rifle-shot at midnight ; but the revolution goes its own way, if silently, then with swifter steps, and breathing fuller strength.

We are yet far from the worst, and this fact we shall most wisely admit without reserve, for, not by looking to the mildest quarter of the horizon, can any captain, as the gale quickens, derive inspiration and for-titude, or devise safety for himself and the rest, but by gazing straight into the eye of the tempest, and watching sea and sky where the storm-symptoms are blackest.

A stone loosened from its site upon a mountain-top may be checked in its first or second revolution by a boy's hand, whose descent ere long no strength can arrest. In Ireland the stone which Michael Davitt set rolling might have been stayed in the begin-ning, though, may be, but for a season, which now rolls irrecoverable to the abyss.

That stone lay there quietly, its uncertain tenure hardly noticed during the whole century; but, inch by inch around it, change and time, descending rain and lashing wind, washed down the earth and rubble in which it lay embedded, until at last with the impulse of a single hand, it was launched from its ancient lair. The stone is the landed aristocracy of Ireland, once firm-rooted on the crest of the hill; the rain and lashing wind are the unrecognised, unadmitted growth of the Irish Democracy, and of ideas thence generated, gradually permeating millions of minds, steadily sapping and wearing away all that which once kept Irish landlordism firm in its high place.

What we now see passing around us was prepared from afar, and all but inevitable. It is idle, and worse than idle, to lose time and breath in the denunciation of individuals. One of the great natural laws by which nations change, is now working out its will over this Irish nation. A storm whose causes lie far deeper than the perversity, selfishness, greed or ambition of any man, or any number of men, blows over the land to-day. All things conspiring to that end, Democracy has

arisen in this country, impelled forward by
its consciousness of youth, strength, and as-
sured victory. With it are numbers, force,
will, and political power. It is a true nurse-
ling of these modern centuries, and its parents
are around it supplying nutriment and support. How, I ask, *can* the Irish aristocracy
finally withstand this younger power, which
has already stripped it of the only effective
weapon of offence and defence in these times,
viz., the Parliamentary representation of Ireland ? Whoever holds that holds all ; he is
master and ruler, though his rule and mastery
may not yet be fully felt ; he is the heir and
has the title-deeds, and those who withstand
him not wisely, will hurt themselves. This is
one of the facts which must be recognized,
and fully acknowledged ; just as a ship's crew
will not forget or ignore the quarter from
which the wind blows. After the next general
election there will be at least ninety Parliamentary representatives of the extreme popular party in Ireland, all or nearly all pledged
Parnellites. I say, therefore, that those
members of the Irish landlord party who

continue to act and speak as if any virtual or real power still remained with us are obstinate and headstrong men, who will ruin and dissipate the now slender chance enjoyed by the Irish landed interest, that namely of making their escape with their pecuniary interests preserved from a situation in which even a little folly will inevitably result in the loss of all that they possess.

That revolutions revolve slowly at first is proved by experience. From the meeting of the States General to the destruction of the Chateaus of the French noblesse, and the flight of the landed interest of France, ruined exiles, across the border, three full years elapsed. Old habits, ideas, and associations, are not dissipated in a year, or for several years. The classes against whom the storm is brewing—whose destruction is all but a forgone conclusion, have always, as if by the arrangement of some Power merciful and just, a full opportunity presented of evading the danger, though madness and blindness, as invariably, seal their eyes against the coming wrath.

And yet the French noblesse, walking their high, strait, giddy path, with a famished people hungering for their substance on one side, and national bankruptcy, a yawning gulf, upon the other, had nothing like the splendid opportunity presented to the land-owners of this country during the first twelve months of the Land League agitation, who, if they had on the right hand a hungry people, had yet upon the left, flushed and abundant, the public credit of a great empire. Had we met the overtures of the League, we might during those months have effected such an arrangement as would have enabled the bulk of our number to have retired from the situation without pecuniary loss. Did even a section of the landed interest respond then to their overtures, hold parley with, or make proposals to the leaders of the people?

A reasonable offer would have been then gladly accepted by the peasantry. Popular imagination, fed by custom, tradition, association, and the undeniable evidence supplied by innumerable acts of legal power, invested territorial proprietors with an imaginary strength. In the general mind their rights stood then firm and unremovable, like the mountain-chains of our country—rights which to-day more resemble hillocks of shifting sand, which yields beneath any passing foot which the wind scatters abroad. The greed inherent in all revolutions, when the very nature of property becomes obscured, and why any man should own anything, a question everywhere arising—the fierce animosity against England's garrison, bred of the expectation that its downfall would soon be— the universal lawlessness, the people's consciousness of unapprehended strength, the vindictiveness, the sense of wrong and outrage at the arrest and confinement of leaders, the madness and headlong movement were as yet unknown. Irish land was still a security for money, and the ministry could have been persuaded or coerced into the arrangement. The pressure of our aristocracy upon the House of Commons, and especially in the House of Lords, could have turned the direction that way of Mr. Gladstone's purpose, and set his financial genius in motion. I remember distinctly the *Times* discussing the proposal favourably, and maintaining that for such an operation the then present was a good time. We had the opportunity, and we let it pass. What reason is there to suppose that the same dim vision, the same dulness of hearing do not now too prevail in our class, that we do not apprehend to-day the real magnitude of coming troubles just as badly as we then miscalculated the swift march of untoward events, of the rush of calamity which has since come? In truth there is none. Even now the dash of waters against the walls, the noise of the disruption of foundations, sound far off and dream-like in the drowsed ears of men slumbering in this house that is built upon the sand.

All too ambitious hopes must be dismissed. The perils with which we are engirt are so many and so ruinous, that only the utmost wisdom and circumspection, and the utmost courage, quickness, and determination, with the adoption of wholly new counsels, will avail to save from destruction a class, without them wholly and irretrievably doomed.

As illustration of the enormous power possessed by a revolutionary and discontented people over a class, even when the latter is backed by over-weening military force, consider the possible and probable difficulties involved in the effort to break up the No Rent combination, and to enforce an even temporary and sullen acquiesence in the law. While the temper of the people is still in that intermediate state in which it will yield rather than suffer eviction, the law indeed triumphs, though at what a cost, what a mortgage upon the future! But suppose that it has reached that point of obduracy and desperation at which it will not yield. Suppose that the peasantry resist the law up to and after eviction, and that estate after estate is cleared out in consequence, the population meanwhile encamping on the borders or upon farms necessarily exempted from eviction, and of which the rent has been to that end paid. Then comes the real tug and strain, estates idle and unproductive occupied by Emergency men, an average of one man to each farm, and at an average cost of 10s. a day, while the landlord remains liable for rates and taxes, annuities, and the interest on charges, besides the initial law costs, which a people who have screwed their pugnacity and determination to such a point, will find many means of evading, as, for example, by the prior mortgage of their effects, or by bills of sale covering them and legally executed, or by the sale outright of all chattels, and their conversion into cash.

Suppose an estate of 220 tenants charged to half its value, and whose rental is £6,600 a-year. Let us proceed to evict it, and count the cost. Twenty tenants pay up, that their farms may serve as camping ground and points of vantage for the rest; the remainder are evicted. The initial law costs are £2000, to start with, incumbered landlord's liabilities £3,200, rates and taxes £800, emergency men an average of one to each farm, at 10s. a day, including hire, food, incidental expenses, &c., £100 per diem, or £36,500 a year. Thus for one year the landlord, or the landlords' combination, for it is plain that the work is beyond the power of any individual to spend on this small campaign £42,500. Why, two or three such estates would exhaust any fund which, for this purpose, the landlords might form.

Therefore, I say deliberately, that the "No Rent" movement, if the people voluntarily or through terrorism go out rather than pay, constitutes a difficulty which is, so far as I can see, insurmountable.

Moreover, be it remembered, that if the landlords proceed to extremities, as indeed if things go on as now they must and will, upon the one side, the people will proceed to extremities on the other. Those Land League hunts—thousands of men suddenly appearing and disappearing, will aim at higher quarry than hares and rabbits, until the gentry, compelled to fall back under the protection of the military, and to assemble for mutual protection in camps, relinquish their houses and grounds, and the land which they now actually farm, to the tender mercies of lawless mobs. In that event we lose those tens of thousands of scattered points of vantage now so invaluable, and the open country remains in the possession of a people too wary to fight, and too determined to succumb.

To overcome all this needs such an executive as it is doubtful whether, in these times, any Government can furnish, least of all, the Government of which Mr. Bright and Mr. Gladstone are the chiefs. In short, to put down a combined and desperate population is by no means the easy task which some persons are in the habit of representing it; and be it remembered, that the No-Rent movement is but an abnormal form of an agitation whose normal and constitutional development is in itself sufficient to secure the end at which it aims—viz., the complete destruction of the Irish landlords as a class, and the confiscation and abolition of all their rights, even their pecuniary rights. For, let it be supposed, that a landlords' combination of a really strong and vigorous character has been formed, and that by its courage, persistency, and determination the No-Rent manifesto has been neutralised, and the tenants universally compelled to obey the existing law. This barrier once passed, we stand face to face with an Act of the Imperial Parliament, by which the rental of Ireland will be cut down by at least a fourth. No combination of landlords, no courage and resolution can ward off that deadly blow ; how deadly every man must be aware who is either himself a landlord, or who has friends or relatives in that position. I know myself many families who will be utterly and irretrievably ruined, and doubtless the tragic list will be mentally increased by each of my readers as he peruses this passage. In an uncommercial country like Ireland, with long-descended families, whose incomes are derived from rent alone, charges of all kinds inevitably multiply, and in the majority of instances, just to that point which enables the landlord, by economy and care, to live with a certain seemliness, and fulfil the duties of his position without general re-proach. A considerable proportion of Irish landlords, small and great, belong to this class.

All whose charges and necessary outgoings amount to three-fourths of the rental of the whole will, with their families, be turned adrift upon the world, ruined, hopeless, and homeless, many of them middle-aged and old, therefore incapable of starting afresh in any capacity. Even the young man thus ruined is far worse circumstanced than one equally poor belonging to a lower stratum of society. He has received no training of any kind which would enable to shift for himself, and by the labour of his limbs provide himself with subsistence. Even as an emigrant he will need some capital which, as a rule, he will not have, for we may be perfectly certain that while a hope, or shadow of a hope remains, he will still cling to the land of his birth and the estate of his fathers, in anticipation of some more fortunate turn of the wheel, until all that is lost which he might have at first realised in cash, and started with as capital in a new land.

But this is not all ; perhaps, indeed, the greatest numbers of the ill-starred yet remain. Those referred to are the men whose estates are charged, or burthened with necessary out-goings up to three-fourths of their rent-produce ; but, even of the remainder, a large proportion are doomed as they. Prior to the agitation, Ireland passed through a period comprising three bad harvests, up to the present succeeded by two years of fierce agitation, growing every day more fierce. I have supposed that the utmost to be hoped for from the combined and resolute action of landlords has been effected, and that the tenants' league has been overborne and conquered. This, however, is plainly a work of time and money; and if the landlords will conquer they must subscribe all they can, and endure a further rough time of at least a year, though more probably of two years. It is therefore apparent, that by January 1, 1883, the Irish landlords will have passed through a period of six years, during which their estates have been but partially productive, and that charges, debts, and demands of all kinds will have accumulated, while even the prospective rents of their estates will have been reduced by a full fourth. Therefore, in the first breath of enforced and treacherous calm, the mortgagees and chargeants long-forbearing will, themselves pushed by the

keen sting of necessity, call upon the judges
of the Landed Estates Court to sell, and their
call must and will be attended to. But what
will be sold, and what will be the price paid ?
The property brought under the hammer will
be not estates, but mere rent-charges—rent-
charges accruing from a disorganised and
deeply disturbed country, and paid by an
angry and revolutionary people, for the moment, may be, cowed by the strong hand of
of the law, and by physical force, but whose
power though latent has been proved too
demonstratively to be hastily forgotten. The
reduced rentals of those whom six disastrous
years, and the unavoidable pressure of mort-
gagees and creditors, shall have forced into
the Landed Estates Court will be sold at half,
or a third of their real value.

How many of the families of our landed
aristocracy will escape the brunt of this deso-
lating storm ? Few and far between they will
appear like the scattered peaks of a sub-
merged world, or like the charred stumps of
the greater denizens of the forest, all of whose
lowlier brethren the wide-wasting conflagra-

tion has destroyed. Yet in the physical world such charred stumps are hewed down by the woodman, who before gathered his timber on the outskirts of the forest. Their humbler brethren were the protection of the great. As surely as the Irish Democracy, assisted by the cynicism, ignorance, apathy, and the growing Republicanism of England, strikes down the rank and file of the class, so surely will it turn its mingled wrath and cupidity upon those proud men who now fondly may imagine that they will escape the fury of the conflagration, scathed indeed but undestroyed.

For there is another more immediate and perhaps more terrible danger, threatening the great as well as the small. May it not be that the charred stumps too will disappear, that all may perish in a single death. Let it be remembered, that socialism, as a formulated scheme of human society, is now some thirty years abroad in the world; that, from Germany, its birth-place, fostered by numerous powerful influences in sympathy with and proceeding from the very genius of the age, it has crossed the Atlantic, and that, recrossing the Atlantic, it agitates the minds of men here in Ireland to-day. Embracing, in its full theory, the whole domain of human life, it has yet, with regard to the Irish land-question, concentrated itself upon the effort to solve that problem at least, in harmony with its own peculiar genius.

According to Mr. George, the author of " Progress and Poverty," whose works are far more widely read and studied than we in England or Ireland are willing to admit, the land of any country belongs, as of right, to the whole people, and therefore the rents—the fruits— are justly claimable by the State as the representatives and trustees of the nation. We require no revolution to accomplish this, he argues—" Transfer all public burthens gradually from personal to real property. Tax land up to its full letting value, and the result is achieved. The essence of the feudal system, from a financial point of view, *i.e.*, the liability of the land for all public expenditure, is thus restored, industry becomes unfettered and free, and earth-hunger, now a curse, will become a blessing. The higher the rent paid the better for the whole people, for that rent is expended upon them, or for them."

It is plain that the enormous, perhaps insuperable, practical difficulties involved in the attempt to realize general socialism, are not involved in this confiscating scheme, and that it directly and plausibly appeals to the cupidity of the landless masses, whose sense of right and wrong, perverted or corrupted by clever writers and talkers, is seldom strong enough of itself to resist the powerful incentives to public plunder supplied by the general hopelessness and poverty of their lot. Let it be remembered, too, that these men thus advised, on high grounds of political philosophy and justice, to appropriate all rent by the simple expedient of taxing land up to its letting value, are no spiritless and nerveless *canaille*, but men wielding, or to wield through the franchise, full political power and authority in this country. As the inducements are enormous, so the difficulties of carrying the advice into practice are proportionally small, and the combination necessary easily realisable.

Thus writes Mr. George, with charming simplicity and irrefragable logic :—

"The political art is like the military art. It consists in combining the greatest strength on the point of least resistance."

"How long would a merchant, a banker, a manufacturer, or annuitant, not to mention the mass of the people, regard as dangerous or wicked an agitation which proposed to take taxation off of him. Even the most prejudiced can be relied on to listen with patience to an argument in favour of making some one else pay what they are paying now."

It would be unfair to Mr. George and his adherents, and seriously affect the purpose for which I have written this book, were I to allow it to be understood that this cynical appeal to lawless instincts, or to the fierce and clamorous appetites involved everywhere in the great social struggle which, for millions, is one for existence, is all that this writer has to allege in defence of his scheme. On the contrary, he first shows that with increasing wealth and civilisation increases, too, in a sort of geometrical ratio, the sum of human misery and vice, and that poverty which is their ancient breeding ground, perennial *nidus* of the ghastly brood.

He then proceeds to demonstrate, or rather assert, the proposition with which we have been only too familiar during the progress of the present agitation, that the land of a country belongs to the whole of the population by which that land is inhabited. Next, he shows how this doctrine is only practically realisable by State-appropriation of rents, arrived at through a land-taxation, equal in amount to the letting value, and he maintains that on the introduction of this reform, the widespread poverty, from which the wealthiest countries are usually the least free, would disappear, or be enormously reduced.

Finally, he argues as above, that it is the interest of those who wield the political power to promote such a reform, and that no effectual resistance can be made by the classes whom the reformers assail.

Now, observe, the doctrine of Mr. George, that the land of a people belongs to the whole people, has been and still is, the watchword of the Irish Land League agitation, and observe also, that not the farmers only, but the whole mass of the population have projected themselves into this movement with an energy and enthusiasm which would be inexplicable but for the presence of some such powerful and all-pervading incentive. Doubtless, the word of their leaders, that in the Land League movement the dream of " Ireland a Nation " was approaching to actuality, exercised a great influence, but beside and around this lay, too, the mightier influence penetrating deeply into every mind, especially of the poor and unpropertied, that those magic words—the land is the property of the nation— meant remotely material good to themselves, a thought dim and vague, but with the power latent in all hopes thus veiled and indistinct, and gradually acquiring formulation in distinct and defined conceptions. The strength of the Land League does not, and never lay, in the farmers themselves, but in the circumabient population of which they were but a part, and on whose enthusiasm they were borne forward. It was they chiefly who formed the great mass meetings of 1880 and 1881, and it was they who sustained and enforced that iron discipline, essential to the League's success, and of which boycotting and outrage were the punishments.

The fact is, that the idea, " the land for the people,"—an idea sustained by consenting influences, the product of the century, and ascending into prominence through the peculiar social and political condition of Ireland— has, through the agency of the *Irish World*, popularising here a portion of German socialistic philosophy, seized the democratic imagination with such tenacity, that the leaders must give to it some practical fulfilment, or retire to make room for other and more daring spirits. The *Irish World* has been in circulation here for several years, spreading its peculiar light in every nook and corner of the land, and though the full meaning of its doctrines are not grasped by the mass of the people, yet they are by intelligent, ambitious, and desperate minds, that is, by minds naturally formed to lead others at all times, and especially so in an age when revolutionary ideas are in the air, and when all traditional and customary conceptions as to the nature of property have been disturbed, and have lost their solidity and definiteness.

I believe that to nearly all my readers the danger to which I here refer will seem too visionary and remote, the robbery involved too flagrant, and the means at the disposal of those who aim at such an extreme measure of confiscation too inadequate, for any such contingency to form portion of the *data* out of which our own leaders must deduce their policy. But let it be remembered, that in revolutionary periods all ideas are in a state of fusion, and that even now, the inherited notions on the subject of property subjected not yet to the hottest fire, have lost much of their solidity and hardness. Menenius Agrippa would find it difficult to turn aside modern socialism from its path by the repetition of his apologue of the belly and the members. Tradition and custom, not˙ philosophy, are the chief defences of property.

Yet, this much at all events is certain, that the solution of the Irish land question is rendered more difficult and more tardy by the prevalence in Ireland of Mr. George's doctrines as to land, now that the whole population, not the farmers only, demand a voice in

the settlement of the Irish land question, re-
quiring a settlement which shall not be in the
interest of the farmers exclusively, or in the
interest of the farmers and the landlords combined. In this matter we have not to deal
with the tenants only, but with all the rest of
the people as well. Thus, a longer vista of
agitation is opened. The path becomes more
tortuous and uncertain. An early settlement
of the question is precluded, and the evil
genius of the landlords will have further scope
and time to rain his blows upon that remnant, not so fortunate as they imagine, who
shall have safely run the gauntlet of the Land
Act, and weathered the storm prepared to
burst when in the Landed Estates Court the
hammer once more begins to fall.

Thus, deep yawns beyond deep, and while
the great territorial proprietor clings fast to
the edge of the precipice, saying, perhaps to
himself in consolation, " My fall at all events
can be only *so* far ; I see the ground which will
receive me"—a clearer vision reveals the fact
that the ground so seen is not level, that it,
too, slopes at such an angle as forbids the

thought that any rest may be found there, that it, too, slants down into dark and hitherto unsuspected gulfs.

The great territorial proprietor who may be tempted to regard his less fortunate brethren in this crisis with a mere sentimental pity and concern, had best remember that, in all revolutions, no great property is safe, and that in this Irish revolution, a doctrine is abroad to-day leavening the minds of that sovereign people which will in a very few years be the arbiter of his fate, teaching them that his possession is an usurpation, that his income is a piracy on the rights of the nation, and that his rents are the property of the State. Let it be remembered, too, that the stone loosened from its place on the mountain's brow, whose course a pebble, a bush, a yard of level ground can impede, ere long in its headlong descent clears at a bound tableland which might afford a resting-place for thousands of its size. Of times like these, of movements such as that inaugurated by the League, can it be least said *experientia docet*, or the past explains the future : for the pace every moment increases, is doubled, and quadrupled, and what has happened, or what men's thoughts have been, indicate not at all what will happen, or what ere long men's will be. Of this, at all events, we may be sure, that the wolf of democracy, which has ravaged the territorial fold in spite of ban-dogs and shepherds, will not, when all protectors have been put to flight, continue long to spare the fattest of the flock. No exceptions can be made. We all row or drift in the same boat, great and small, on the same running tide. We all near the same rapids, in whose spray that fills the air we are each one even now immersed.

Nor must it be forgotten at all by those who in our interest would act wisely in the present crisis, that the genius of this revolution, which from our side appears a monstrous compound of cupidity, fraud, and wrong, seems to the mass of the people of this land a very angel of light, an incarnation of ever-lasting Hope, new-risen at length with healing and salvation. The revolution which over us rolls with grinding and destructive force, is to

them Ireland's winged and flashing chariot,
in which she passes at last to her avatar—a
nation among the nations of the earth. It is
no vulgar appeal to cupidity by which we are
solely or chiefly confronted, but one framed
with consummate skill, which, while sup-
ported by the base desires of the base, stirs
also the deepest and most passionate instincts
of man.

To the mass of the people the Irish Aristocracy appear as the deadly foe of the Irish
nation—a foe which eighty-one years since
sold to England the independence of their
country and their own great future as the
leaders of a nation, for a paltry sum of
money, or for still paltrier baubles and trap-
pings, and exchanged, for ignoble sloth and
abject, uneventful lives, a career of high effort,
beneficent activity, and glorious responsibility.
To them our class has ever since presented
itself as the chief and most potent engine by
which England has enslaved and fettered her
sister, free-born as she. They hate us because anti-national, and despise because anti-
national for such mean rewards. The day of

absolute democratic power in Ireland draws nigh—the day of reckoning and vengeance; while through half-shut eyes we look out and murmur, " It is all well ; England is bound to protect us."

But England is not bound, does not regard herself as bound, to see us safely through these thick-coming troubles, in which, as in a net, the Aristocracy of Ireland is now fast caught. Nay, the better opinion is that England herself is moving forward swiftly upon the same tide of democratic change which in Ireland has borne us to that point at which to-day we hear, not so far off, the thunder of waves against those fatal shores, where better crafts than ours have often split before. The England that we know is swiftly transformed even while we gaze. The Crown and Coronet have lost their lustre and magic power. There is no charm in them, as of yore. Cade and Frost, long immured, or lurking in obscure places, are out once more, with power a hundred-fold increased, no longer talking vain things or laughed at by the wise, but girt with all the strength of civilization, with science and political philosophy in their train, and the English democracy at their beck. Cade is now Premier of England, with men like Spencer and John Stuart Mill for his mad preachers, and the doctrine that sixteen shillings shall pay a pound he has actually enacted as law in Ireland, and with the approval and sanction of the Imperial Parliament, of the Throne, and of the English people.

England, it cannot be too often repeated, like a rotten staff, will break under the weight of the Irish Aristocracy, if, while it totters, it leans once more on that old support. England has slowly, bit by bit through the century, transferred the political power here from us to our enemies, and has sanctioned and encouraged the agitation. which has led us thus far on the road to ruin, and to-day appears as the originator and maintainer of a law which smites into the dust the larger number of a class once her trusted and trusting ally ; and through her responsible leaders, laughs at the notion that any reparation is due to those whom her policy has ruined. Of

political power we have lost all but a remnant,
and that remnant melts before our eyes like
stripes of mountain snow. The grand juries
will go like the corporations, and the unpaid
magistracy will follow. The suffrage will soon
enclose the whole people, if that is now to be
regarded as a loss; while the Land Act,
combined with the revolutionary disturbances
which England cannot or will not suppress,
sweeps away utterly the material substructure
upon which the very existence of the class
was built.

Let me repeat myself. We at this moment
are confronted by two deadly enemies, the
Land League and the Land Act. The latter,
perhaps the deadlier, still dallies and lingers
—his blows are as yet scarce felt : the other
has already closed with us. Granted that by
courage, combination, and wisdom, we subdue
by force the Land League—a result which
depends on a contingency *—there remains
the other foe not to be subdued, for he is in-
vulnerable. He is the strength and might of
the British Empire, so armed as to laugh at

* See pp. 11, 12.

our blows, while his own are fatal. The conquest of the Land League, if haply it may be conquered, merely brings us face to face with this other deadlier foe.

The result, then, at the best, will, for the Irish landowner, be, on the one hand, a Democracy subdued, couchant, biding its time for the next spring; and on the other hand, England, represented here by the Land Act, having smitten himself to the ground, emptying his pockets of nearly all that he possesses, with sanctimonious professions of justice and sanctimonious homilies on the unrighteousness of his career.

What proportion of the landlords of Ireland will be ruined outright in this land of heavily-charged estates, by the abstraction of four millions from the rental of the island, I cannot say. That two-thirds in number of the class see in the Land Act their own doom pronounced, is not, perhaps, too much to assert, if we include amongst them those so impoverished as to feel that emigration is their wiser course. But all these are so much strength torn from the side of the surviving landed interest. They are men to whom nothing is left, nothing to fight for, no inducement, once their new rents have been adjudicated, to spend time and labour and incur anxiety and peril for the continuance of strife on behalf of the rest. If they leave the country, they are lost to the class; if they remain, it will be with aims and desires far different from those which they now cherish: aims and desires whose nature England may yet dearly rue.

Of the remainder, another two-thirds, pressed upon by the effect of six disastrous years of mingled distress and agitation, will enter that valley of shadow and shame, through which, never to return, many of the oldest and noblest families of the island have already passed. The League still couchant, unsatisfied, ready for war, who will purchase their rent-charges at the commercial value? The Judges of the Landed Estates Court, pressed by clamorous creditors and mort-gagees, themselves sore stricken, will, as was done before in the Court for Encumbered Estates, sell them out at ten and twelve years' purchase. Each applicant will get a small slice of the very attenuated and shrunken loaf; the owner will go out hungry, with the world before him. The remaining ninth must try conclusions as they can with the sovereign people. Some may indeed survive, but few and far between, lifting no serene heads above the tossing waves, *rari nantes in gurgite vasto*. As a class, the Irish landlords, their offshoots, scions, and collaterals, their agents and dependants, their flatterers, and all who in any way ministering to them bore the same mind and the same social, religious, and political bias, will have disappeared, sunk for ever, like last winter's Channel wrecks, scarce noticed, scarce pitied, amid the newer waves and storms of this stormy Irish sea.

But compensation! Has not the *Daily Express* taught us that compensation from the Imperial Government is our right; that for rents arbitrarily and for State purposes reduced, the State, the benefiting party, must make full and ample remuneration, and has not the claim been endorsed by the assembled landlords of Ireland? Is not England a just and Bible-loving nation, and has not English justice passed into a proverb? Can she withhold from us this patent right? Have we not in this country been England's garrison and right hand, and for her sake incurred the hatred of our own countrymen, and aroused thereby the chief part of the vindictiveness with which we are at present pursued? and will you now, O England! destroy and extirpate us from the land of our birth—a land dearer to us in this trouble than we had ever deemed that it could be—vainly hoping to appease thereby our enemy and yours? You would bribe the Irish Democracy to enter the Union, but the cost of the bribe you filch from us, your friends. You hope to suborn this people into surrender of its cherished birthright with a mess of potage; but, worse than the patriarch, you first steal from your friends what you offer your enemies as a bribe. But beware how you stir up the fierce hostility of men conscious of a wrong so deep!

To all which, one who has read recent Ministerial speeches, and is aware of the genius and policy of the English Liberal party, can imagine that the Premier thus replies:—

"Now hearken to me, O Irish landlord: You talk of justice and right, and of incomes arbitrarily taken away. Your rents have been indeed reduced, not by despotic acts of power, but by the arbitration of judges and valuators selected chiefly from that best class which intervenes between you and the tillers of the soil, who as between man and man have adjudicated for you fair rents, and I have no proof that those judges have not honourably and conscientiously discharged their duty. The Land Act was sanctioned by Imperial Parliament, in order that in accordance with its provisions, fair rents might be determined; and though, misled by statements, both I and my colleagues were under the impression that the existing rents were fair, they have been now proved to have been unfair.

"If I grant compensation as a right, then I insult the tribunals which I have set up, and charge with corruption the gentlemen whom I have appointed judges. Compensation and

reparation are due only for property taken
away. But you have lost nothing, for the fair
rent fixed by competent persons is all that
you are entitled to under the Act, and, as you
appeal to justice, all that in justice belongs
to you.

"And remember this, too, O Irish landlord,
that you have already taken and enjoyed out
of that Irish soil, wherein we first set you,
and since upheld you, more than the blindest
justice can condone. I have read in the ex-
cellent works of Sir Henry Mayne, that the
Celtic tenures of that island protected the
tenant from arbitrarily increased rent, and
secured him in the enjoyment of his improve-
ments, and, therefore, of such enhanced value
as, with the general growth of prosperity, might
accrue to the soil. But you, having entered
into the lordship of the isle, not through your
own might but through ours, took to yourselves the absolute and irresponsible dominion
over the soil. You imposed what rents you
pleased upon a people whom we laid prostrate
before you, you swallowed up in rent every
improvement which the labour of your serfs

might effect, and you took to yourselves the whole of the enhanced value of the soil which accrued to it during the present century, owing to the growth here in England, and through English genius, of a great industrial population, a result to which in no way directly or indirectly did you contribute. With rent you stripped your country to the bone, failing not to extract, too, the marrow. Therefore, talk not to me of reparation and compensation, when your own people, the nation amongst which you are but a class, without power and without repute, calls out with a voice, not cricket-like as yours, but with a voice of power that from you to them is due such compensation as the whole rental of your estates cannot make good. Take what you get, though a remnant, and stir no awkward controversies. As your wings must be clipped, you flutter and struggle at your peril. Decapitation, not the loss of a few superfluous feathers, may be your reward. Therefore beware.

"Your allegations of ingratitude, too, and of services rendered in times past are still vainer. Who else planted you in that Irish soil but the power against which you raise now your objurgations and complaints? We for you suppressed the great rebellion of 1640, spending English blood and treasure that you might be happy, and for you conquered Ireland in the Jacobite wars. Since the ships that bore southwards—never to return—Sarsfield with his Irish regiments and the exiled remnant of another aristocracy, dipped below the horizon, have we not kept from your eyes even the sight of any enemy, encircling Ireland with our fleets and armies, as with walls a garden, that you might take your ease therein, and gather such fruits as your slaves might plant? And whenever we heard your voice calling for help against their mutinies, and discontent, did we not respond with armed help, reducing them once more to their sullen thraldom? Nay, did we not at the beginning of the century, at your appealing cry, occupy the same ourselves, and rule and order all things therein, you having grown weak, incapable, and if the truth be confessed, somewhat dastardly, permitting you to retire to pleasant arbours, and eat the more abundant fruit which our wiser management and other circumstances conspired to produce, or to walk and take your pleasure there without labour on your part, and without responsibility?

"Listen yet again, O landlord! You in that Ireland of yours, which, after all, is not yours but ours, have ceased altogether to be what once you were, and you will not understand or acquiesce in the change. Your serfs are no longer serfs, but free men, having votes, wielding that power which alone in these days shapes legislation, and directs policy. The whole political power of your island has passed, or is fast passing, into their hands, and their stress and strength is already felt in the Senate, in the central *officina legum* of this Empire. Your friends, men of like minds with you, have even here grown feeble, and your enemies have grown strong. Democracy here, too, rises like the sun potent and irresistible, of whom I am the herald. Moon and stars, the Throne and the nobles, wax paler every hour. I would rule and regulate—why should I not? and to my rule were I to grant you all that your hearts desire, what could you contribute? Those who have risen against you have power and strength. Their aid I need, and in my own way, I seek to acquire. You are nothing—the shade, maybe, of that which was once strong, but is now dead; which at the cock-crow, heralding a new day in the political and social life of your nation, disappears with a cry.

"And, as to Imperial generosity, and such large munificence as becomes great States when ruined and fading classes call for aid, look you now how unreasonable is your demand. Know that of all taxation, no matter where placed, the brunt and weight falls at last upon the overburthened shoulders of the labouring poor. You ask for an annual four millions to recoup your loss. How can I appear before my own people—a people themselves distressed and perplexed by years of disastrous harvests, with diminishing trades, with silent factories, and furnaces black and cold, while over all, like a mountain ever-nodding, looms the vast impending mass of a debt without parallel in the annals of man, how, I say, and with what face can I appear before them, and repeat all that I have now said to you, and add, 'Yet, my generous countrymen, let us for these ruined men and their families, as a great act of Imperial munificence, provide by Act of Parliament out of our own resources, an annual four millions, and save them much suffering, and add to our own renown.'

" To tell you the truth, my Irish friend, I would not, even if I could, lay any such monstrous burthen on my already sorely overladen people, millions of whom, even now, hear around their own homes the baying of the famished wolf. For justice' sake I might try, because justice and righteousness are my delight—would that they had been yours! but as a deed of munificence and generosity I cannot, and were I to attempt it, I know well, too, what a scornful answer I should receive."

To which our spokesman in this ideal dialogue, driven by hard necessity, might thus reply :—

" O Premier ! we question the accuracy of your logic, and perceive the limited views of your statesmanship, especially in that passage in which you contended against the justice of compensation. But it is vain to argue with the master of many votes, therefore we perforce forbear. Yet consider now this suggestion which, if adopted, will both save us, and lay no additional burthen on your people. Of the two mill-stones tied around our necks, whose weight will drag us down into the depths, the most grievous is not that fastened by your unjust and wrongful hands, but that imposed by hard necessity and fate. I refer to the heavy charges and encumbrances with which we are each and all over-weighted. Grant now an imperial loan of money, which you can raise at two and a-half per cent., that we may buy up these encumbrances, and let the substituted debt remain a perpetual charge upon our estates, we paying for it the same interest that you pay to the lenders. We would thus save an annual two and a-half per cent., for at present we pay five. Or if you will, let it be three and a-half, of which one per cent. will form a sinking fund, in time to absorb the whole.

" Or again, purchase from us our estates, as many of us as desire to sell, at a fair price, say twenty, or twenty-two years' purchase of the average paid rental for a period of fifteen years preceding the agitation. The Imperial credit here again will avail, not only to give relief adequate, or nearly so, to the landlord, but to keep the public resources unburthened. Moreover, by such an arrangement, the farmer thus converted into tenant to the State, would pay a rent much less than that at which even the sub-commissioners will assess him.

" For example, the average old rent to which a farmer was liable is, say, £20. This at twenty years' purchase, is £400—the sum to be paid by you to the landlord as purchase-money of the fee. The interest on this sum at two and a-half per cent. is £10, which, imposed on the lands as a quit-rent for ever, will be just half the original rent. The sub-commissioners would probably not reduce his rent below £15. If it were considered desirable to insist on annual payments towards a sinking fund, there is thus an abundant margin for that liability."

To whom, looking askance, the great tongue-fighting Premier :—

" Hearken to me now once again, and for the last time, my astute Irish friend, badly financial with a cunning purpose. Your rents, you know well, you cannot henceforward re-cover without trouble, loss, difficulty, delay, and expense, if even then. The position which you find untenable, or deem it prudent to relinquish, you would knavishly persuade the English people to enter, you escaping scot-free with the full money's worth of your territorial interest, an interest all but drowned in the revolutionary tempest which a just Pro-vidence has let loose against you—a merited penalty for your greed, your fatal blindness, and obstinacy. Your lands lie right in the path of a descending deluge, against which my moles, and dams, and coercions, though wrought with enormous expense, and all on your behalf, I fear much, though brazening out as I may, will yet prove quite ineffective. Moreover, that minor rush which I permitted in order to ease the pressure from behind, and that which perforce wrought its way through

and over, has saturated and sore damaged a
security always bad, and now worthless. To
be frank with you, my knowing friend, I will
not lend the hard-earned millions of my people upon your rotten security.

"Let the country return to peace and tran-
quillity. Let love of order and of law be restored. Let all debts, including chiefly your
rents, be paid with regularity and without
murmuring, sedition, or crime for a period of
three full years—let the Irish popular party,
soon to control the whole Parliamentary representation of your country, and regulate so
much therein, desist from their insane hatred
of England, and act in every way as if your
island were an integral portion of the British
Empire, and when all this has been accom-
plished, call again, and I promise that though
three courses may then, as usual, present
themselves, I, possibly, circumstances conspiring, may not, as it were, be disinclined to
adopt that course which, at the same time
holding out hope to you, shall best harmonise
with the prosperity and happiness of this
Empire, and the advancement of liberty and
civilisation over the whole world."

" Thank you for nothing, O kind Premier ! In the event you mention I, or whoever then shall hold my diminished rents, will, in a peaceful and settled country, sell them in open market, and for a better price than financial genius sitting on the Treasury Benches, and delighting in good budgets, is likely to advance."

I crave my reader's pardon if I have displeased any by trifling at all with the gravity of this crisis, whose terror and gloom I feel equally with the most troubled in this island, not to any serious extent for my own sake, but for that of many friends and relatives, and the thousands of homes whose daily life and habit of thought and feeling I know so well, and understand without witnessing, and for the sake, too, of the future of this land and nation. The preservation of Irish landlords as a class, though divested of territorial power, the wise statesman looking only to the welfare of the country, and unaffected by personal sympathies, would most wisely risk everything in order to accomplish. On this ground, if on no other, I most ardently

desire the preservation of that class, noblest
and best on Irish soil, to be, and to be felt
and known to be, the highest moral element,
the light, the ornament, and the conscience
of the young barbaric power now ascending
in our land, of this fierce, dark, vengeful democracy, soon to be let loose with all its
savage instincts uncontrolled—a protection
and covering of the new birth forming in Ireland's womb, the caul of the infant Republic—
smoothing the passage between caste and
equality, softening, healing, consolidating,
mitigating, preserving and transmitting to
new generations the social ideal as this
younger birth, trumpet-tongued, comes pro-
claiming the political—grace, courtesy, refine-
ment, moderation and modesty, politeness,
and its greater parent kindness between man
and man, sensibility and personal pride, as
the other louder, not nobler, comes with its
own, liberty, love of country, national pride,
far-reaching national ambitions and aspira-
tions.

If in the foremost ranks of Irish democracy
there are statesmen not mere *revolutionaires*—

if there are men who ride and guide the
storm, not waifs and straws, rolling things
borne blindly on its breath, they will with me
see the terrible responsibility, the great duties
which have devolved upon them in this solemn
crisis of their nation's history. This I pre-
dict, with the same assurance that one might
in Autumn the approach of Winter, that the
extirpation of the Irish aristocracy now de-
creed by the combined power of a cynical
and time-serving Government, the pressure
of unrelenting fate, and the turbulence of a
fretted and untaught people, will, at all events
after the fulfilment by the Irish democracy of
their ideal—Independence—be succeeded in
due course by an Ireland gross and material-
ised, falling prone before the first glittering
idol which the times will present. One knows
well what that idol will be.

All history is a lie if this be not true, that
successful Republics adore mammon beyond
any other imp of the devil's brood, and most
rejoice to sacrifice before his altar with filthy
rites. The remains of the feudal civilisation,
the influences subtile, undiscerned, yet power-

ful, emating from a class in which wealth and
rank, long inherited and taken as matters of
course are, therefore, slightly regarded, combined with national poverty, national suffering, and the consequent pursuit of ideals that
appeal to men's more rational nature, keep
down now the uglier manifestations, the more
shameless profession of this vile cult.

That democracy holds deep in its soul lofty
ideals, yet in some favoured land and time to
be realised in institutions, and practically in
the lives and characters of millions of human
beings, I believe; but equally true it is, that
aristocracies struck down are replaced by
plutocracies, and that the social influence of
noblemen and gentlemen is succeeded in due
time and invariably by that of vulgar wealth.
In the interest of democratic republican Ireland, if for no other reason, I call upon the
people's leaders to beware how they press
beyond recall a class, the costly product of
centuries, containing elements of moral, personal, intellectual wealth, which this nation
will yet sorely need, and which, with all its
gifts, and with all circumstances consenting

and conspiring, it cannot again of that kind ever produce.

Is there no hope, then, for Irish landlords save in the possible growth of the sense of justice and right, of statesmanlike and far-reaching prudence in the popular party and its chiefs? Plainly, if in policy our future resembles our past, there is none. Those who will not row, or steer, or set their sails, observing how the wind blows, and the tides run—who merely drift with the tide, and run before the gale, will sooner or later meet their doom. Have we up to date formed a policy? Have we even realised the necessity of forming a policy? Is there any formulated line of action into which, urged by public spirit, and the instinct of self-preservation, we can project our energies? Do we see, or has any one shown us, the vantage-ground which once seized, no matter at what cost, we may dominate the field, or where we may intrench ourselves and gain breathing-time for the next advance? No. Who are our leaders? To whom do we, the rank and file, look for the word of command? They have not been selected. Have we even said to our Parliamentarians—seventeen in all—no inconsiderable knot in the House of Commons—" Stand together for us. Preserve your independence of the English Conservative Party. Compel them to make our rights the basis of their party action, and neglect this duty at your peril." We have not, though it is apparent to all, that without pressure these will be necessarily sucked into the stronger current of a great Imperial party. Have we, as a class, done anything, planned anything ? We have not. Have our principal men planned anything ? If they have, I should like to see it.

Therefore, I say again, we neither row, steer, nor set sail. We drift.

We look to England, and say with Mr. Micawber, something will turn up. But it wont.

Look rather at the Land League, the iron discipline, the organisation, the self-reliance, the marvellous astuteness and courage of its chiefs, the never-failing plan, always the pursuit of a definite line of action marked out by the leaders, endorsed by the rest.

Why then have I written this book if I have no hope to offer, no line of action to suggest? Simply to prove to Irish landlords that if we proceed as we are proceeding, our fate is decided; and if any one should call me an alarmist, I shall be pleased, for I wish to alarm!

STANDISH O'GRADY.

11 FITZWILLIAM-STREET,
DUBLIN.

www.ingramcontent.com/pod-product-compliance
Lightning Source LLC
Chambersburg PA
CBHW031804090426
42739CB00008B/1151